Good Mornings

Wake-Up Calls for Life

by

Dr. Randolph D. Sconiers, DSW, LCSW

Printed in the United States of America

First Printing, 2016

Second Printing, 2018

ISBN: 978-1-7292-5262-8

Good Mornings is a book of inspirational and motivational morning messages to help you start your day. I started writing daily good morning messages several years ago, and started sharing them with others via social media. I realized from the responses that mornings set the tone for the day. A wake-up call is used to keep you on schedule, so that you don't miss a beat as you take on the day. *Good Mornings* provides wake-up calls for your life, and helps you stay on schedule as you pursue your purpose, interact with others, and grow as a person. The messages are easy to read, and I provide practical strategies to support each message. I use these messages to set the tone for how my day will flow, and I believe people will greatly benefit from these powerful messages of hope, reflection, and inspiration. Please share these messages with others and encourage them to get the book to begin their path of Good Mornings.

<u>How to Use Good Mornings: Wake-Up Calls for Life.</u>

Begin each morning with a Wake-Up Call, or a passage from the book. Throughout the day, focus on the message, and work on taking action steps to support the call. Use the *Good Mornings: Wake-Up Calls for Life* book every day until you have finished all the Wake-Up Calls, or completed the entire book. Then you may go back and review specific Wake-Up Calls that have resonated with you. You may also challenge yourself by opening to a random Wake-Up Call and meditating on it at any given point in your journey. Lastly, it's just great to share *Good Mornings: Wake-Up Calls for Life* with others in order to help them get on a positive path of purpose. Make sure you encourage them to get their own as well!

Good Morning,

HAPPINESS, FREEDOM, AND PEACE ARE all active processes that require a conscious pursuit. We can't be stagnant and believe we will simply wish these beautiful desires into existence. Our ability to choose must be utilized. Our faith must be activated. Our work must be diligent and steadfast. Although our dreams are experiences we cherish and so often share, it's our effort and energy that opens doors. So, match your desire with determination and your expectation with your energy. Enjoy your happiness, freedom, and peace. You worked hard for it!

1. **What does happiness mean to you?**
2. **What does it mean to have freedom?**
3. **Why is peace of mind so important?**

Good Morning,

TODAY IS YOUR DAY. IT's up to you to utilize that powerful weapon called **choice.** Get up and make a choice to be happy, healthy, and purposeful. The power of choice should be your anchor throughout the day, as it keeps you focused if things get off track. Let's hit the ground running, with the power to choose how this day will go!

1. **How can the power of choice change your life for the better?**

2. **What are some areas in which you can improve your physical and mental health?**

3. **Practice positive thinking to keep you on track.**

Good Morning,

TRUST IS A POWERFUL PROCESS and can be incredibly effective in helping you reach your goals. You should begin with trusting yourself, believing in your ability to weather the storms, make mistakes, and get back up with a determined attitude. You should also trust timing. The belief that doors will open on a schedule that's not in line with yours, and it's okay. **Timing** has a way of not notifying us of the "when" of the blessing, but somehow knows the exact point in the journey in which we are ready. Trust is earned and often never given. It's okay to trust yourself. You know how awesome you are!

1. Write down your feelings and thoughts about trust.

2. Write down your feelings about timing.

3. How are both connected in your own life?

Good Morning,

TAKE NOTHING FOR GRANTED. YOUR success should never be measured by material possessions or comparisons with others. **Your value must begin with peace of mind** and an unwavering acceptance of who you are as a person. The possessions can be taken away but peace can sustain you when all is gone. **What defines you?** Your character is what people will remember, so cultivate that aspect of your life with passion. Your respect for others, your kindness toward others, and your resilience during the storms will forever be connected to your name. You are worth more than you could ever imagine. Now walk it and talk it!

1. **What are the people, places, and things of value to you?**

2. **How important is good character to you?**

Good Morning,

CHANGE IS DIFFICULT TO ACCEPT, but necessary for growth. The discomfort you feel is communicating that change is taking place in your life. You may want to return to that place of familiarity, but resist the urge. **Change pushes you**, whether you like it or not. Would you move on your own? Would you step out without that nudge from change? Would you step out in faith and believe you can do it? Next time you think "I hate change," just realize how much you'll "love the results" in due time. Enjoy the change!

1. How well do you cope with change?

2. Why is change so important to our growth and development?

3. What areas in your life are in need of some changes?

Good Morning,

RUN WITH THIS TODAY. **YOU are** more than capable. You don't have to follow the paths of others to be successful. You have your own **ideas, dreams, and goals.** It will not be easy, so eat right and sleep right because it's a marathon that you're running. **Don't worry** about the hurdles--you were born to jump those and you will. I know you have it in you to win, but you must decide when...I believe today's a good day to start!

    1. What are some of the goals you have for your life?

    2. How is your mental and physical stamina each day?

Good Morning,

I DECIDE! I HAVE THE power of choice, which can help me determine the direction of my path. Choice can also be utilized in regulating my mood and how I treat others. A victim mindset sets one on a path of powerlessness and blame. A victorious mindset is a path of determination, acceptance, and choice. It's my power, my choice, and my decision to be happy. I no longer have to be afraid of happiness because I am in control! Today is a perfect day to make this choice!

1. **How will you choose happiness today?**
2. **What decision do you need to exercise today?**

Good Morning,

WHAT IF YOU DECIDE TO put your **purpose over profit**? You go hard to seek and explore the gifts and strengths that make you extraordinary. You're incredible and talented in so many ways, but your most exciting quality is your desire to help others. Purpose is more valuable than any profit you could chase or lose your soul for in this world. Purpose moves us toward peace and happiness as it centers us in a calming way. Make a commitment on this day to your purpose over profit, and move with a focused cause rather than a shallow applause. You are great, and no monetary value can define your worth. P.O.P! Purpose over profit!

1. **Have you explored your purpose?**
2. **We all understand the importance of money, but seek peace as well.**

Good Morning,

THIS IS THE PERFECT DAY to take on a mindset of **faithful work**. This concept simply means, taking proactive steps to put your faith into action. It's the idea of working hard and creating the opportunities. It's making that call, going to that school, or looking at that new business location. It takes your words and activates them by putting strategic energy into that area of your life. I don't believe having faith alone will open a door, or hoping for a breakthrough will magically create one. Faith without works is dead, so conversely faith with works brings new things to life! Let's create some new opportunities and new things on this new day!

1. You can activate your faith by putting forth focused actions.

Good Morning,

How bad do you want it? Your drive must match or exceed your desire for success! There will be long days, tough nights, and sacrifices along the way as you push toward your goals. Don't be discouraged. It's a marathon and you have to be in it for the long haul. Keep your focus and your endurance at optimal levels. You're going to look back and laugh..."I did it." Yes, you did!!!

1. **What's driving you to keep pushing?**

2. **Start planning with short- and long-term goals.**

Good Morning,

FEAR IS THE ENEMY OF success. It has a couple of codefendants as well, named doubt and hate. The great part of it all is that you have superpowers to defeat fear and his henchmen. You have the powers of faith, determination, and love. You need to put on your faith every morning and live like you already own it. You carry determination with you like no obstacle can get in your way. Lastly, you show love to others because you want everyone to win. Help others realize their superpowers by sharing this message today!

1. Don't let fear stop you! You're more than capable of winning.

2. How can you show love and compassion to others on this day?

Good Morning,

IF YOU TRULY BELIEVE IN your passion, it's time to go all in. Shake off any doubt or fear. It's time for you to make those calls, connect with those people, and visit those places you have been avoiding because of possible rejection. Don't fear failure, but embrace the opportunity to grow and go to the next level. I wish you success as you step forward and move closer to your goals!

1. **Write down a couple of action steps for today. Things that need to get done.**

2. **Is there something or someone holding you back? It's time to move on!**

Good Morning,

Is your new season on its way? Sometimes we can just sense it. It's time for a change and it's scary to see ourselves in a new location, on a new job, or around a new group of people, but change often unlocks our next blessing. The idea is to change our perspective on the new season and see the change as a positive process that pushes us out of our comfort zone. We all have experienced that feeling...that "it's time to move on" feeling. Maybe it should be called that "it's time to move up" feeling. Up to the next level! Enjoy the next season in your life!

1. Why is change sometimes a good thing?

2. Do you need to move out of your comfort zone in any area of your life?

Good Morning,

BE THANKFUL FOR THE PEOPLE that push you to be **better.** Sometimes you need to evaluate your circle and assess whether you are being drained and pulled down by people. You're trying to figure out why your feeling tired physically and emotionally...maybe it's the company you keep. Don't be afraid to distance yourself from people who are not providing you with positive vibes. The energy you come in contact with on a regular basis can communicate so much about your current situation. Are you progressing? Are you feeling stagnant? Who's in my circle? Are we supporting each other? Just a few questions to consider when you're checking on your circle. Have fun!

1. **What does your circle say about who you are?**
2. **Are you making progress as a result of your interactions with your circle?**

Good Morning,

IS YOUR LABOR PRODUCING THE results you desire? You should be enjoying the fruits of your labor as often as possible. You put your time, energy, and focus into your work, only to hope that you will yield a desired harvest. When we don't take time to appreciate our work, have fun, and laugh...what's the point? Work on creating more holidays for yourself. A lifestyle in which you have more moments to reflect on your hard work and effort while taking the time to enjoy your success! You deserve it!

1. Do you take time to enjoy the fruits of your labor?

2. What activities can you plan to reward yourself for all of your hard work?

Good Morning,

START TODAY WITH A SINCERE appreciation for life and everything it embodies. Don't be afraid to try something new today. Stretch your confidence and start planning your next takeover. It could be improved health, educational goals, career moves, or that new business plan. It's your choice and you're right to make the moves to position yourself in a better place than yesterday. Every day has the potential to be life changing. Let's see what you do with your today!

1. **List 3 things you are appreciative of and write them down.**

2. **Practice mindfulness today. Stay focused on the here and now.**

Good Morning,

WE RUN FROM PURPOSE AND always seem to run into our purpose! **Why can't we just be still** and live our purpose? It's less tiring that way!

1. **Practice being still today with 15 minutes of quiet time.**

2. **How can you continue to pursue or develop your purpose?**

Good Morning,

YOU'LL HAVE TO BE CRAZY enough to go after your dreams, and caring enough to support others who are chasing theirs! Crazy and caring!

    1. What crazy step can you make today to accomplish a goal?

    2. How can you display more caring for others?

Good Morning,

THERE'S NO REASON TO LIVE in the past. You've already lived that time, made those mistakes, and celebrated those victories. Now it's time for you to live for today and plant seeds for tomorrow. Growth is a gift!

1. Are you holding on to anything from your past? How can you let go?
2. What seeds can you begin planting today?

Good Morning,

TODAY IS YOUR GIFT. YOU may not see it wrapped in fancy packaging but it is a gift to be appreciated. Today is a new opportunity to live, improve, and grow. Let's start appreciating the gift we so often take for granted. Enjoy your gift!

1. **What are you grateful for today?**

2. **What gifts can you share with others on this day?**

Good Morning,

THE CHALLENGES IN LIFE HAVE a way of bringing out some of our greatest strengths. We become hyper-aware of our creativity, patience, and faith. That's why it's important to embrace the rain in expectation of the sun!

1. List some challenges that you have experienced over this past year.

2. How have you developed strength and resilience from these challenges?

Good Morning,

YOU CAN'T SIT AND WAIT **for success to show up at your door.** If you want it, you'll have to put in the extra hours, go new places, and do new things. You must kill the "I'm about to..." mentality and live the "I started and did..." mindset. **Action will be the key factor** that separates those who succeed and those who only dreamed of success. The choice is yours!

1. **What's stopping you from taking that next step toward success?**

2. **List 5 action steps you can take today to put you closer to your dreams.**

Good Morning,

NEVER STOP BELIEVING IN YOUR vision. It's your perspective on a path that was designed for you, and some may never see it that way, and that's fine. The goal is not to get others to see your vision but allow others to see the drive and energy you put forth to catch that vision. I hope you continue to pursue your dreams with a crazy amount of energy and passion!

1. Why is having a clear vision for your life so important?
2. Try creating a vision board. Use pictures and words to describe your vision.

Good Morning,

LEARN THE POWER OF SAYING **"No," and use it.** Sometimes we are so programmed to say "Yes" and continue to neglect ourselves during the most critical times. We must see saying "No" as a powerful tool in the process of self-care. Start saying "Yes" to yourself! You deserve it!

1. Do you have a hard time saying «No» sometimes?

2. List 3 ways you will begin to say "Yes" to yourself.

Good Morning,

I BELIEVE IN MY PURPOSE **and know I will make an impact on the lives of others.** I'm ready to build with like-minded people that are focused on changing the world for the better! Let's connect!

1. How can you positively impact the life of someone else?

2. Explore ways to connect with others in order to change the world in some way.

Good Morning,

IF YOU'RE GOING TO DO it, do it with greatness as the only goal! Don't get lost in mediocrity...average will leave you somewhere in the middle. Do everything in excellence!

    1. What does it take to be great?

    2. Are you walking with a mindset of excellence in all you do?

Good Morning,

WHAT ARE YOU WAITING FOR? Pursue that goal that's inside of you. That thing that keeps you up and distracts you at times. Why are you running away from your purpose? Does it seem impossible? Well, we have seen the impossible become reality. Just look around and see how many incredible wonders have come to life from the seemingly impossible dreams of people that never stopped believing. **Now is the time to step into your next season** with faith, determination, and some hard work. How will you ever know? There's only one way to find out. Go for it!

1. List 3 people who you consider to be great. List some of their traits.

2. What's burning inside of you? What passion keeps you up all night?

Good Morning,

MY STRENGTHS AND CAPABILITIES ARE **ready to propel me to the next level**. Sometimes the only person holding me back is me. Today, I need to write down my 5 strongest gifts and my 5 strongest attributes. I need to post them and review them before I start the day. I then must begin carrying those gifts and attributes with me every day. I must bring them to life and utilize them to create the life I want for myself. I will not let fear stop me, but I will step boldly into accomplishing my goals. **It's my time to shine and I am more than equipped to win!**

1. **Write down your 5 strongest attributes and review them daily.**
2. **How can you activate your attributes in order to move closer to success?**

Good Morning,

LETTING GO CAN BE THE **most challenging aspect of change**. In order to go to the next level, you'll have to leave behind some people, places, things, and ideas. Maybe that's why you're not where you want to be at this time. You keep trying to bring old ways into new dimensions. Those outdated approaches won't function at the heights you're about to travel. It's going to take a new outlook and a new way of movement for you to sustain the success that's headed your way. Be ready, be prepared, but never be surprised! You deserve it!

1. **Do you need to let some things go? What's holding you back from winning?**

2. **Take a stand and proclaim, "I'm moving forward. It's my time."**

Good Morning,

KEEP WRITING YOUR STORY. YOU may have experienced some difficult chapters and wondered about the crazy storylines that keep showing up in your life. It's enough to make the average person put down the pen and concede to a sad ending, but there's nothing average about you. You continue to write and begin to craft the next chapter with some sunshine to push away the clouds from past chapters. It gives you hope and determination to keep the story going. You are living a masterpiece, a great novel, and a story of resilience. Never give up. The story of your life may inspire someone else to keep living their life story!

1. **Write the title of your life story:**

   _____

2. **What chapter are you currently living?**

Good Morning,

THE EXPERIENCE OF FEAR IS simply a test of your faith. Your desire to start a new business, take your relationship to the next level, or make that power move will definitely evoke fear, but so what? We give fear too much power. Our faith is stronger, but we often belittle it against feelings of fear. When we put faith first in our decisions, we know we will win. Our confidence increases, and our actions become hyper-focused on seeing it through. Fear is no match for your faith!

1. How important is faith in your life?

2. Turn down the volume of fear and turn up the volume of your faith.

Good Morning,

IF PEOPLE SAY YOU WILL never make it, just let that go! Some people cosign it, provide the financing, and pay interest on self-defeating statements!

    1. Are you creating or listening to self-defeating statements?

    2. Write down 5 self-progressing statements and read them aloud.

Good Morning,

YOUR NEGATIVE THOUGHTS AND POSITIVE desires are bound to disagree!

1. **Don't let negativity interrupt your day.**
2. **Match your positive desires with positive thoughts.**

Good Morning,

YOUR STRENGTHS MUST BE EXERCISED **and utilized for success.** You may not be scratching the surface of your incredible talents. People may see things inside of you that you are choosing to ignore because of the fear of failure. **Don't be afraid to step up and step out with those gifts** you have in hand. Maybe the key to going to the next level is to use what you already have instead of seeking more from others. Put your gifts to work today. It's your time to shine!

1. **Are you ignoring your gifts and talents?**
2. **What's inside your house? This simply means use what you have today.**

Good Morning,

YOU NEVER HAVE TO COMPARE **yourselves to others.** Many times people feel pressure to keep up with others by focusing on their material possessions, lifestyles, or accolades. This can be physically and emotionally draining. Most importantly, you will never be defined by the accomplishments of others. **Wake up every day with a sense of security** that you will do things your way and follow the purpose that was designed for you. You should never live in the shadows. Be the sun! It's your shine!

1. How can you be the sun and shine on this day?

2. Have you ever experienced being in the shadow of someone else?

Good Morning,

BE BRAVE! NEVER LET FEAR win on your journey to success! Stand up strong and activate that unshakeable faith with ridiculous energy and passion. You were designed to win and prevail against any obstacle that comes your way. Walk like you own it, but keep a humble attitude. You're supposed to be here. Act like it!

1. What does it mean to be strong yet humble?

2. Write down 3 strength-building affirmations to help you today.

Good Morning,

LET IT GO. NOW!

Sometimes we hold on to people, places, things, and ideas that simply hold us back from success. I call them the "**nonsense nouns**." These are the negatives that only bring us down and cause unnecessary nonsense in our lives. Why should you let it go? These "nonsense nouns" occupy your time and energy, which causes you more stress than you need. It's like we're afraid to let them go because we are so used to having them around. The NOW! part is a critical part of this post. There is no time to think about it. 1…2…3, and let it go! You'll feel better right away and can focus more on being happy!

1. Are there any "nonsense nouns" in your life?
2. Make life happier by letting go of _____ .

Good Morning,

THE STORMS HAVE A SUBTLE way of reminding us that life is not about perfection but appreciation. **We need to cherish the sunshine**, even the little moments of sun have value. The day-to-day reasons for being thankful must never be taken for granted or ignored. We don't have to be angry at the storm because it too has a purpose. It has a way of humbling us during the journey but also raising our anticipation that the sun will shine again. Enjoy the weather!

1. Write the names of three people you appreciate. Now call and tell them.

2. What are some things you are thankful for on this day?

Good Morning,

MAKE SURE YOU POSITION YOURSELF for the blessing.
You're waiting for that door to open but maybe you're
in the wrong spot. Maybe you are not ready yet for
what's behind that door and need to change your position to open the right door, at the right time, and when
you're in the right position to receive what's behind
it. 1. Keep working and moving toward your goal. 2.
Align yourself with those who push you forward. 3.
Keep your faith up and back it with focused actions.
You will move yourself in the right position for the
blessing!

1. **Who are the people that push you forward?**
2. **What action steps can you take today?**

Good Morning,

NOW IS THE TIME TO put "it" down. You know that hurt, disappointment, or regret that so many of us carry around every day. It can feel like you are carrying around a large rock that just keeps you from moving forward. One of the ways to be released from your past is forgiveness, and another way is to make peace with your past. Peace comes when we accept we are not perfect and that it's okay. Forgiveness is a verb that requires an active release from being bound by the doings of someone else or yourself. It's time to go to the next level, so let that go! You'll feel better right away!

1. Today is the day to release

_____.

2. Is there someone that needs your forgiveness on this day?

Good Morning,

THERE ARE NO LIMITS ON **this journey!** You can go where you want and see what you want. If we remove the boundaries that typically exist in our minds, we will live wonderful lives. My goal is to travel more and experience more on this journey called life. I hope you will join me on this mission of liberation, and escape from the walls that hold us captive. You deserve to be free!

1. I have the power to create the life that I want and desire.

2. I will choose freedom and peace of mind on this day.

Good Morning,

OUR BEAUTIFUL BLEMISHES AND FASCINATING flaws make us completely correct!

1. Write down 3 of your flaws and 3 of your blemishes. (Be honest.)

Good Morning,

IT'S TIME TO SPEAK HAPPINESS **and success over your life.** When you verbalize positivity over your life, you begin to walk as if those processes are true. You begin to believe that you are stronger than the negative energy you may encounter throughout your day. The most powerful and important part of using this formula is to match it with your actions. Walk with your head up, show kindness to others, and encourage people throughout the day. Create the life you want and put out energy you want in return. Peace and Blessings!

1. Speak 3 positive words over your life.

2. Check your energy level. Do you need to replenish your reserve?

Good Morning,

NEVER UNDERESTIMATE YOUR ABILITY TO **be creative in a crisis, or your tenacity during turmoil.** We all have strengths that we can tap into during tough times. Our creative flow allows us to consider all options and ideas to remove ourselves from the storm. Our tenacity is closely tied with our determination, faith, and hope to push through the storm. I believe in your creative mind and tenacious spirit. Never give up!

1. How can you show creativity during a crisis?

2. What does the word determination mean to you?

Good Morning,

EVERYBODY WANTS TO FLY, BUT nobody wants to crawl, walk, fall, and get up again. **Success is a series of steps, failures, and comebacks!** Never forget it!

1. Stay the course. Endure the ups and downs to meet the goal!

Good Morning,

YOU ARE STRONGER THAN ANY **obstacle and more than capable of doing extraordinary things!** Believe in yourself and appreciate the support you have from others. It's time to go to the next level!

1. Be strong today in the face of any obstacle or challenge.

Good Morning,

PEOPLE CAN FEEL YOUR ENERGY **and get a sense of who you are in a matter of seconds.** Your aura communicates for you, and before you utter a single syllable, people already know. When there is a conflict between your vibes and your words, people begin to question your authenticity. Something isn't right and you know because they know. **Make sure your walk and talk are synonymous.** Be your authentic self. The other stuff doesn't really matter.

1. What kind of energy do you express in the presence of others?

2. Do your actions match your words? Work toward harmony.

Good Morning,

PERFECTION DOESN'T EXIST BUT ITS **presence is powerful.** It pushes people to modify who they are in a quest to obtain that which will never be conquered. Maybe a better goal is peace. There's a quietness to peace that's much more calming than perfection. Peace is a profound acceptance of self and the journey designed for you. It's okay to chase your dreams and push for something greater, but if it's perfection you're after... choose peace instead! You'll enjoy the feeling!

1. Do you have peace in your life? How can you obtain more peace?

2. Don't be so hard on yourself. It's okay to fail and learn from the experience.

Good Morning,

SEE TODAY AS A NEW **opportunity to change the world.** How many lives can you impact in a positive way? In what way can you deposit something beautiful into the atmosphere? Our collective positive energy is powerful enough to make this day something incredible. Let's get to work!

1. **How can you impact the world in a positive way on this day?**

2. **Make a positive deposit into the atmosphere.**

Good Morning,

YOU HAVE GIFTS AND TALENTS that can transform your life and help others as well. The key is exploration and observation. We live in a very cookie-cutter society where emulation is considered the best road toward a successful destination. I believe we lose pieces of ourselves in trying to imitate the lifestyle, movements, and journeys of others. This trip or process must be our own. We deserve to have our own downs so we can pick ourselves back up, and our own highs so we can pull up others. Be you! The world will appreciate the original!

1. **Help someone in need on this day.**
2. **Be your beautiful self on this day.**

Good Morning,

If you're going through some major changes in your life, it can feel really scary. You'll have a desire to go back to your comfort zone, but remember why you needed that change. It's not easy to go to a new place or start something all over again. Many people never take that leap because of fear while others just can't stay in their current place because their comfort zone is killing them. Maybe it's emotionally, maybe it's mentally, or even physically killing some people. The everyday stress became too much to bear, so you decided to embark on this new journey. You are resilient enough to endure the growing pains of change, so be strong enough to never give up!

1. Don't be afraid to move out of your comfort zone.

2. Write down 3 strategies to combat negative stress in your life.

Good Morning,

ARE PEOPLE TALKING ABOUT YOU? Are you facing an increase in the level of hate being thrown your way? Does it seem like you're facing some crazy obstacles before that door is set to open? Maybe you're on the right track! The closer you get to the next level of blessings, be prepared to face the next level of blessing blockers. Don't give up or be defeated because you're closer than you think to that blessing! Keep your head up, faith strong, and actions focused on winning. The tested will tell a testimony of trials but triumph in the end!

1. **Don't respond to negativity being thrown in your direction.**
2. **Walk with your head held high at all times.**

Good Morning,

KINDNESS CAN BE CONTAGIOUS. IT seems that little acts of kindness can create an avalanche of beautiful gestures. Imagine a world where everyone committed to one act of kindness a day. Each act would transfer a powerful energy to the person impacted by the act, which could lead to even more acts. Let's decide to start the kindness chain. Wait until you see the chain reaction!

1. **Show more kindness on this day.**
2. **Start the kindness chain on this day.**

Good Morning,

SUCCESS WITHOUT PEACE IS REALLY not success at all!

Good Morning,

Don't allow yourself to be in a waiting or reactive mode in regards to your goals. You have to be proactively working toward them on a daily basis in order to see the results you want. The smallest step can open the biggest door, and your blessings may start pouring in. Try it!

1. Be proactive on this day.

2. Write down one action step that you can take toward your goals.

Good Morning,

BE CONFIDENT IN YOUR ABILITY to overcome the day-to-day challenges and life stressors. Take a minute to reflect on your resiliency. Do you remember the last time an obstacle seemed insurmountable and you pushed through with an unshakeable fight? That's the same strength that can help you conquer any hurdle that comes your way. I believe in your fighting spirit! Keep going!

1. **Believe in yourself on this day.**
2. **Keep a positive attitude on this day.**

Good Morning,

RUN WITH THIS NEW KNOWLEDGE **today.** Move in your own direction. Stop compromising and conforming to be accepted by others. Hit the reset button every morning. That means you have another opportunity. Stop chasing material possessions, because in the end nobody cares. I would be more impressed if you gave it away to a just cause. It's time to redefine success. **You are successful, loved, and valued.** Never forget that!

    1. **What does success mean to you?**
    2. **Give yourself a mental reset. Meditate on a peaceful place.**

Good Morning,

YOU DESERVE TO BE HAPPY **but that doesn't mean you will never face difficult times.** Many times we are being prepared and tested based on the size of the blessing that will follow. The precious piece of coal is pressured, heated, and tested before we ever call it a diamond. In its beginning stages, it's still a diamond!

1. Pressure is used to create diamonds. You can handle the pressure.

Good Morning,

Monday is a day that is often criticized because it symbolizes the return of the workweek. It's all a matter of perspective. Monday also symbolizes a reset or a new beginning. It's an opportunity that should never be taken for granted. It's a chance to set the tone and flow of the week ahead. What if you try to move into your Monday with some positive energy and focus? You may see the rest of your week follow Monday's lead. Let's not be so hard on Mondays. It's whatever you allow it to be! Make it great!

Good Morning,

It's time to embrace the idea that you are multi-talented and multi-gifted. Why should you limit yourself or your capabilities? I'm in total agreement that you should never put all of your eggs in one basket. Your goal should be to use your strengths to create multiple baskets and fill them with many different types of eggs. Then take the time to help others with their baskets as well. The idea is to see yourself as an individual who is capable of doing extraordinary things, and someone who can help others along the way. Let your gifts shine today. You have so many, why not use them? I believe in you!

1. Look in the mirror and repeat, "I am gifted and talented."

Good Morning,

WE MUST CONTINUE OUR PERSISTENT **push on our own terms with the focus of never giving up in the face of challenges, obstacles, or hurdles.** Our persistent push should be a daily mantra and way of living. Our vibes should remain positive while understanding the world will present us with negativity. Let's move forward and accept the challenges that come with success, and embrace the learning that comes from failing. **Our resiliency is our strength.** We will forever push with a powerful and purposeful persistence!

1. **Never give up or lose sight of your goals.**
2. **Be resilient!**

Good Morning,

PEACE DOES NOT COME FROM **receiving sympathy or validation from others.** Ultimately, peace comes from forgiveness, letting go, and moving forward. When you have internal quiet and external comfort in your journey. Make this day a peace-seeking day. It's a powerful process and a beautiful thing to have peace of mind. Enjoy!

1. **Create more moments of peace on this day.**
2. **Take time to quiet your mind on this day.**

Good Morning,

THIS JOURNEY CALLED LIFE WILL **present us with challenges, obstacles, and hurdles that are designed to bring out our inner-most desire to overcome.** We shouldn't be moved by the mountain, but instead we should consider strengths we have to move the mountain. We all have strengths such as our spirituality, family, friends, and our resiliency to push forward. Let's begin to embrace the challenges that make us stronger and know the tested ones are the blessed ones!

1. Be strong in the face of challenges.

2. You have to be focused and faithful. You will win!

Good Morning,

YOU EVER LOOK AT A **journey and wonder if success is really meant for you?** We all have days where we question our passion and purpose. This is normal and I believe necessary on the road to success. It's called "evaluating the plan," and should be done continuously. It's a proactive approach to measuring progress, areas of need, and focus. Don't be discouraged if things are not moving fast enough--you'll get there. Trust the timing!

1. **You will be successful.**

2. **Don't rush your blessing, be patient and persistent.**

Good Morning,

THE CLOSED DOOR!

Why do people look at the deal that fell through, or the door that closed as such a finite event? Sure it's disappointing, but we should never be driven by the direction of the door. We should remain driven by our purpose, passion, and faith to continue regardless of the closed door. In fact we should start to approach life with the mindset of embracing closed doors as "not my blessing." This only means that your blessing is behind a different door, a much larger door! One door closes and two others may open. Stay driven by your determined desire...not the door!

1. What will you fail today? Failure is a sign of risk and learning.

2. One door closes and another one opens.

Good Morning,

IF PEOPLE GET OUT THE car on your journey to success just expect to get there much faster! Not everybody is down to ride the whole way!

1. Some people will step away on the journey. That's okay.

Good Morning,

HOW ARE YOU AT SAYING, "No?" Sometimes we take on the weight of others or find ourselves adding more to our plate that we can handle. I wonder if your kindness and caring genes keep you from saying "No." That's okay, you've said "Yes" more than enough times, so don't feel guilty. This is the time to practice saying "No," so you can recharge your own battery, work on your own goals, and say "Yes" to yourself. Practice saying "No" today when you're faced with something you're just not feeling. Watch and see how much weight is released just by saying "No."

1. Saying "No" is a good self-care strategy.
2. Say "Yes" to yourself.

Good Morning,

DON'T BE YOUR STRONGEST ENEMY. Sometimes we are fighting and battling against ourselves and it's negatively impacting our ability to move on from our past. We let our past experiences with hurt or issues with fear, advance into our strongest ally or our greatest enemy. The idea is to side with our thoughts and use them to defeat the negative attacks against us. Focus on the positives in your life. Think about how blessed you are to have another day to live. Keep positive people around you to create more support and encouragement. Do your best to keep the energy that radiates from you positive and focused. You're more than equipped to win! As long as you think it, believe it, and live it!

1. Keep your thoughts positive and strong.
2. Look in the mirror and say, "I am strong, successful, and peaceful."

Good Morning,

SOMETIMES WE EXPERIENCE TIMES IN **our lives that feel like we are traveling through a dark tunnel with no light at the end.** We may become doubtful that we will ever overcome the hurt, disappointments, and obstacles that always seem to pop up. I want to encourage you to never give up or stop pushing. Your strength is your resilience and determination. You've already overcome challenges that would have made others throw in the towel, but you're still standing. It's time to get in thriving mode and turn off surviving mode. You are more than a survivor. You're a champion already! Keep pushing to win!

1. Let your light shine in times of darkness. You can make it through.

2. Time to push forward. There is no time to hesitate.

Good Morning,

FEAR HAS NO POWER. ITS strength is fictitious and created by doubt, negative thoughts, and perceived threats that are false. We have the ability to defeat fear through our most powerful weapon, our mind. Our thoughts impact our actions and can push us to overcome fear, but we must be steadfast. We can't waiver or allow any doubt to creep in, or fear will believe there's a chance to triumph. Be victorious over your fears because you already have the victory! Just start to believe it!

1. Don't feed the monster of fear. It can't defeat you.

2. You are stronger than your fears.

Good Morning,

BE APPRECIATIVE OF THE JOURNEY. The ups, downs, and curves. Don't forget the unexpected exits, moments to refuel, and those so important rest areas. There's also something special about the people you meet along the way. Some you remember forever and others you can't wait to forget. You'll of course have happy moments as you try to patiently wait to arrive at your destination. The key is not to become hyper-focused on that final destination, but be mindful that the journey eventually comes to an end. So live, laugh, and love...enjoy this adventure called life!

1. Get ready for the ride of your life. You're on a great road trip.

2. Get off the path and take a break. It's important to rest up.

Good Morning,

GOING AFTER YOUR GOALS AND **catching your dreams
can be a scary process.** The thoughts of failure, doubt,
and ridicule may enter your mind with the hope of
derailing your plan. Don't let these enemies of success
stop you! Your determination, faith, and passion to
succeed will not be sidetracked. You have a desire to
capture your dreams and the discipline to fight until
the end. Put on your uniform of faith and match it with
your undeniable action. Let the words "I will succeed"
become your new motto. I'm excited about you getting
to the next level!

    **1. I know you can accomplish your goals. I be-
lieve in you!**
    2. Be determined to win!

Good Morning,

WHEN WAS THE LAST TIME **you checked your account?** I'm not talking about your bank account. I'm referring to your circle account. When was the last time you checked to see what kind of things people are depositing or withdrawing from your life? Are the people in your circle making deposits of love, hope, faith, and pushing you to be your best?! Do you let people withdraw negatives or positives from your words and actions? These questions are designed to make you think and assess your circle, in order to go to the next level. Make sure you do a monthly check of your circle account...maybe it will impact your bank account! Either way, you'll be happier!

1. **Is your circle hurting or helping you?**
2. **Do a circle check!**

Good Morning,

BE THE BEST "YOU." WE live in a society that's driven by competition and social comparison. People often measure their success against the success of others, which can leave people feeling inadequate or extremely arrogant. The best formula is to challenge yourself to be the best "You" on this journey called life. This approach leads to a sense of peace, which is far more powerful than the pressures of keeping up with others. It sounds cliché now, but the concept of "Do you" is much more valuable than some may think. It's an affirmation of strength for people who are working on themselves versus worrying about being judged in the spotlight of others. Be you!

1. You are awesome!
2. The spotlight is on you. It's time to shine.

Good Morning,

IS IT WORTH IT TO ignore the daily blessings and gifts we have in front of us for the desires we hope to chase and to obtain? Only you can answer this question but be mindful about neglecting the people, places, and things that are of real importance as you chase dreams. The love of family and friends is priceless. The benefits of good physical and mental health should be cherished. The gift of peace of mind is a present that can never be replaced. The rat race can have you going crazy for material possessions, just remember to put it all in perspective. None of it really matters! Live, Love, Laugh!

1. **Enjoy the little blessings. None of them are really little.**
2. **Self-care is critical to good health and wellness.**

Good Morning,

SAY GOODBYE TO ANYTHING NEGATIVE that has rented space in your mind. You are the owner of your thoughts and feelings. You have the right to serve eviction notices to doubt, insecurity, fear, and depression. Maybe it's time to serve notice that negativity has to go immediately. You'll enjoy the new freedom that comes with a clear mind. It's called peace!

1. **Time to kick out the negativity.**
2. **Now you have more room for happiness and peace of mind.**

Good Morning,

SET PRIORITIES AND ELEVATE YOUR value to reflect your worth. You don't have to settle in a world that often becomes content with mediocrity. It's more than your right to demand the best. If people are not bringing something of value to the table, maybe it's time to do some circle cleaning. I want you to start walking and talking like greatness in all you do. It's not arrogance. It's acceptance of your true excellence. Put others on notice! You're top shelf and only those who reflect that aura can ride with you!

1. **Reflect on your values.**
2. **Demand the best. Why should you settle?**

Good Morning,

SUCCESSFUL PEOPLE ARE TESTED. THE stretching of your patience, and the pressing from tough times activate your fight. Your ability to get up after a knock down is great, because you've been knocked down before. You appreciate winning, because you know what it's like to lose. You're humble during success, because you know what it's like to fail. Never give up during difficult times. Just keep your head up and push through!

1. **The test will lead to triumph.**
2. **You will be knocked down but never allow yourself to be knocked out.**

Good Morning,

WHAT ARE YOU WATERING AND Feeding?

Sometimes there are things growing in our lives because we are watering and feeding them. That water and food gives those negative monsters energy to create chaos in our lives. Don't nurture hate, doubt, and fear. Make sure you're not setting the table for anger and depression to chow down on your relationships and goals. It's time to close that restaurant down! Starve the negativity and you'll get full off of the positive energies happening in your life!

1. **What are you feeding and watering?**
2. **Grow more positivity.**

Good Morning,

THE LOVE IS NOT ALWAYS the Same

We put love in the atmosphere and hope that it will be returned with the same intensity. We quickly realize that's not always the case. Sometimes people have a hard time reciprocating the love you give because their heart is in a different place. Maybe there is bitterness or anger toward your ability to show love so easily. The worst thing you can do is let that stop you from continuing to show love to others. If the energy is meant to be returned, it will flow back to you. If not, you show it anyway. Love without condition can change a person, change a mind, and change the world!

1. **Love is in the air. Take it in.**
2. **Show unconditional love and watch it return.**

Good Morning,

TODAY I WILL CHANGE MY **narrative.** I will decide how I want this day to be. I refuse to let negative self-defeating energy occupy or invade my circumference. I will choose happiness, success, and productivity today. I will speak kindness of others. I will let go of anything and everything that disrupts my flow of greatness. Mondays will never be the same. I'm ready!

1. Write your story with an honest faith that you will win in the end.

2. Your story is not over. Keep writing.

Good Morning,

DON'T WORRY ABOUT TRYING TO keep up with everybody else. The gram (Instagram) will have you convinced everyone is a millionaire mogul, traveling the world, Bentley driving. Just live your purpose and follow the path that was designed for you. You'll soon understand that the smoke and mirrors is never worth the stress! Live, Love, Laugh!

1. **Don't follow the crowd. Follow your own path.**
2. **Keep up with your own goals and dreams.**

Good Morning,

IF YOU'RE MISSING THE MARK, maybe you're trying too hard to keep up with the crowd. Create your lane, expand your lane, and stay in your lane. Your authenticity will shine through!

1. Create a lane that represents your gifts.

Good Morning,

Your past: A reminder of your strength, courage, and resiliency. The moments that provide the opportunity to reflect on the times that made us smile, and those occasions that made us cry.

Your present: A gift that's current. The motivation to act now and push for our goals with an unwavering energy and determination. The idea that we should love today, and appreciate every moment that we are actively living.

Your tomorrow: The motivation. Our dreams and desires. That reason we go so hard. Our hope and future. That awesome day that inspires us.

Good Morning,

IF YOU LET FEAR SET **up residence in your mind, it will slowly take down every picture of love, success, ambition, drive, confidence, passion, and purpose that lives in that space.** It will also gladly open the door for its friends doubt, depression, and anger to stop by and take room as well. The point is this—don't let it in. Let fear know from the door there's no space available, and then slam the door!

1. Give fear its eviction notice.

2. Move love, confidence, and purpose into your life on this day.

Good Morning,

Trust the Timing

We want to see changes immediately and that's not always the case. There is something special about trust as it relates to timing. It's complete security in the designed unfolding of whatever will occur. There's a sense of peace when you don't have to force or rush what will happen. You can continue to push forward with a strong belief that everything will work out according to plan. Just say, "No worries, I'm good." Yes you are!

1. **Don't rush it.**
2. **Be patient but active.**

Good Morning,

THE POWER OF EMPATHY

Putting yourself in the shoes of someone else is a lost art. There's a powerful connection that takes place when we try to feel what someone is feeling, and experience what someone is experiencing. It changes our perspective and brings us right into the narratives of others. We develop improved clarity and a better understanding of the journey that others are traveling. We need more empathy in this world. Let's give a little more!

1. Practice empathy by listening and feeling.

2. Put yourself in the shoes of someone else on this day.

Good Morning,

Your Character Arrives Before You

Before you even step foot in the room, your character has already arrived. Your name, reputation, and pedigree are already in position to help or hurt the situation. It's important to leave positive pieces of you along your journey. Leave incredible impressions that will communicate, "Someone great was here." Your character will arrive before you and set the atmosphere for relationships to develop, goals to be accomplished, and happiness to spark. Make sure your character allows others to anticipate your arrival and not pray for your absence.

1. What does your character communicate about who you are?
2. Be a person of integrity.

Good Morning,

<u>The Rare and Endangered Trait Called Kindness</u>

When we spot it, we are often in shock and surprised by its presence. We often associate its proximity with some ulterior motive or an attempt to gain some sort of leverage. Kindness seems to be headed toward extinction in this get-out-of-my-way, no-time-to-lose, instant-gratification society. That's both scary and sad, as future generations are not seeing this rare trait as often as needed.

There is hope. If we can begin to show increased kindness whenever possible, it will reproduce and show itself more in public. It's possible we can see this trait make a comeback, and once again we can enjoy watching the phenomenon called kindness!

Good Morning,

Know when to walk away. Sometimes our season is over and change is beginning to take place, but we can't let go. Change is uncomfortable, so we resist it. We refuse to embrace that our time with that person, place, or thing is over. Maybe we are afraid of what's on the way, or maybe the unknown makes us nervous. It's best that we listen to our inner-voice and prepare for something new. We might just like what the new season has to offer.

1. Walk away from the negativity that's impacting your life.

2. Move out of your comfort zone!

Good Morning,

You're in control of what you allow your ears to hear and eyes to see. It's your right to change the channel, or move on from anyone or thing that's making your mind restless. There may be family and friends in your life that have good intentions, but once in a while you need to adjust the volume of their feedback when it comes to your life. Sometimes you need to reduce the volume when the words are negative or antagonizing. There are other times when you need to turn the volume up on people that are pushing you to win and persevere. Lastly, we have the mute function. Just mute people that try to tear you down. The mute button can be used for quick silence and peace when needed. All three functions can help at any time!

1. **Be mindful of what you allow your eyes to see and your ears to hear.**
2. **Find some time to be by yourself. Give your mind some rest.**

Good Morning,

NOTHING IS MORE PAINFUL THAN **hearing the truth.** I'm not talking about criticism disguised as truth and created for ill intentions. The truth I'm referring to comes from you. It's knowing that you need to make some changes, but it hurts to think that you allowed yourself to be that way for so long. The truth is vital, and the pain is necessary. There is no growth without stretching, and no progress without the pain that pushes us out of our comfort zone. The truth hurts, but living a lie is death compared to the pains of being honest with yourself. Be truthful to yourself, because you're strong enough to take the pain.

1. The truth allows you to grow and progress.

2. Don't be afraid to make some changes in your life. Change for the better.

Good Morning,

<u>Give up? Never!</u>

If you wanted to throw in the towel, you would have done it already, but that's not you. You get tired and beat down at times from life's battles, so you're tempted to give up the fight. Suddenly, a surge of energy reminds you that you're not the type of person that will stay knocked down. Your strength to pick yourself up and battle that situation is inspiring. The life you have experienced feels like something made for the big screen. The trials, tests, and triumphs...starring you. That's because you're just not the type to give up. Believe in yourself, believe in your fight, and believe you will win in the end.

1. **Giving up is not an option.**
2. **You are stronger than any obstacle.**

Good Morning,

<u>Activate Your Dreams</u>

Today is the perfect day to push the action button on your dreams. It's time to put the energy, focus, and planning into those deep desires that keep you up at night. Watch out for hate, fear, and doubt. We call them dream assassins. It's not enough to have dreams and park them in some empty lot in your mind. It's time to get those dreams going by activating the engine or plans that will have your dreams running like fine-tuned machines. It's up to you, so get started!

1. **Push the action button on your dreams.**
2. **Start today!**

Good Morning,

When you follow the strategic design for your life or your purpose, it's a beautiful journey. This path supersedes those other things society deems as necessary when choosing a professional commitment. This is about happiness, freedom, and peace. That's what your purpose gives you. Everything else comes as a result of pouring your time, faith, and passion into that thing, which only you can do. It only gets better when passion connects with your purpose. It's a fire-like energy that drives your purpose forward. It's a lethal combination for success, happiness, and peace of mind. Find your purpose and add in some passion, a recipe for greatness!

1. **Your passion drives you. Your purpose guides you.**
2. **Follow your purpose with passion.**

Good Morning,

LIFE LESSONS BUILD CHARACTER

I have a special appreciation for those who have been challenged in life. There's something about people of resilience and fortitude. It's the classroom that so often gets overlooked by society. It goes far beyond grades, degrees, and accolades. I respect the toughness and determination of the person who has been knocked down but never knocked out. Life is the greatest teacher, as it builds discipline, patience, perseverance, and resiliency. I don't believe we give enough credit to those who have pushed through hard times, battled cancer, conquered poverty, or who simply go hard every day to put food on their table. Let's salute the students of life's school. No graduation date, no certificates, but tremendous character is forever obtained. Salute to you!

1. **Life's challenges make you stronger.**
2. **There is strength in your resiliency.**

Good Morning,

<u>Kill Them with Kindness</u>

They're expecting you to return the hate, but you have a better idea. You could access and use the same weapons they spray at you, but you're on another level. You came strapped with something they never expected. You're going to kill them with kindness. You are about to send the opposite energy into their direction and watch them stand confused and dazed. Your kindness screams you are bigger and better than the hate being thrown at you. It's the ultimate weapon for the haters. They just can't take it!

1. **Avoid giving out negative energy. Keep positive vibes in the air.**
2. **Don't let the haters lead you to using hate. Be love.**

Good Morning,

Don't Be Afraid to Shine

Sometimes we run away from happiness and success. It makes us uncomfortable to be in a position of peace because we may have experienced so much chaos. We carry the dark clouds with us long after the storms have passed. Today's a new day. It's your turn to step into the spotlight. You deserve to experience the shine. You have to believe in yourself and embrace the glow. **The glow symbolizes someone who has experienced some storms but stepped out again with the shine of a new season.** A new opportunity and attitude. Let the world see you shine today. It's your time!

1. What does happiness mean to you?
2. You have the glow!

Good Morning,

I'm a Work in Progress

I'm a work in progress. My story is not complete. I have so much more to live, and people I want to meet.

My narrative is lengthy with moments full of pain, but I'm a work in progress with so much more to gain.

There are chapters of triumph and chapters full of tears. Chapters of confidence and moments full of fears.

My story is still ongoing, so there's no need to drown in stress. I have a journey still to travel. I'm a beautiful work in progress.

Good Morning,

Give Your Dreams a Chance

Many say there is no great reward without great risk, and this mindset works well for your dreams. Sometimes you have to close your eyes and just give your dreams a chance. If you look around, you will back out. If you listen to what others have to say, you will back out. These are your dreams, ambitions, and keep-you-up-all-night thoughts that never seem to go away. It's up to you to give your dreams a chance to develop, grow, and flourish. Take the risk. You never know what the reward may be!

1. **Never give up on your dreams.**
2. **Make a dream board as a visual reminder of all of your awesome dreams.**

Good Morning,

A LOVE LETTER

I needed to write this letter to let you know how special you are to me. Sometimes I need to show you and put time aside to appreciate the value and blessing you are to others. In the past, it was hard for me to say the words "I love you." I had a hard time believing this world truly cared for you, so I followed that lie.

Through some tough times and harsh battles, you never gave up on me. That's why I needed to write this love letter to you. I finally realized something so important. In order for me to love someone else, I needed to love me first.

That's why I'm writing this love letter to you. The "you," I'm referring to is me. Always remember to love yourself. You deserve to be loved by you.

Good Morning,

I'm perfectly fine. My beautiful blemishes and fascinating flaws make me completely correct. I love who I am.

1. Repeat, "I'm perfectly fine."

Good Morning,

STAY FOCUSED!

There will be distractions from every direction when you're pressing toward your goals. The distractions come in the form of negative people, negative thoughts, and everyday stressors that over-occupy your attention. Sometimes you need to have tunnel vision and walk the path with hyper-focus. You'll get things done as always, but practice with effective, efficient, and effort-driven energy today. Today is a great day to stay focused!

1. How can you stay focused and free from being sidetracked by distractions?

2. Remember these words today, effort, efficiency, and energy.

Good Morning,

You are greatness, and should move in with this mindset. When you form a partnership with greatness, it radiates out of you, and will leave evidence of your presence as you travel. It's not about competition or titles. This is about you putting your all, in any area of your life in which you desire to be excellent. Greatness is achievable because greatness is you. It's just time for you to walk and talk in the greatness you are!

1. **Be great in all you do!**

2. **Look in the mirror and repeat this, "I am greatness."**

"Active Your Dreams"

Step 1: Answer the Call!

You are being called to do something great, but you keep ignoring and declining the call. Your dreams are calling you every day in various situations but you're avoiding picking up that call and responding. Now is the time to answer and get to work!

Step 2: Courage

You will have to **show an enormous amount of COURAGE** to see your dreams come true. Don't allow yourself to be discouraged by doubters, haters, or dream killers. Be bold and move with determination in order to get closer to that dream.

Step 3: Today

What will you do **TODAY** to make your dreams become reality? The idea that you can wait until tomorrow is false. You need to take little steps each day toward that which you desire. Today is a powerful idea, as it focuses on immediacy and present action. Activate your dreams now by taking strong action right now!
Today!

Step 4: Invest

You need to make **INVESTING** in your dreams a mandatory process. You have to put in the extra time, energy, and focus in order to see the results. When others are backing out on your dreams, never worry or fear. This is a sign that you need to increase the level of investment in your own dreams. Now is the time to INVEST!

Step 5: Vigilant

BE hyper-aware of your circle and the company you keep. Activating your dreams will bring you in contact with various people, places, and things. It's critical that you're mindful of those systems that will try to bring you down. Vibe with positive energy and listen to your senses for danger. Be Vigilant!

Step 6: Ambition

There is an inner-drive inside of you that can't be seen or explained by others. It wakes you up every morning with a "nothing can stop me" mindset, and a determination to see your dreams come true. It's a positive and powerful force that combines your faith with action until the goal is reached. The power of ambition allows you to jump hurdles and run through obstacles for that dream. Show your ambition on this day and every day!

Step 7: Time

The process of accomplishing your dreams is more like a marathon than a sprint. It is critical that you maintain "active patience," which is very different from waiting. As you continue to work hard on your dreams, utilize patience to give you peace during the journey. The time that it takes will make you appreciate the journey so much more. Time is not your enemy, just use it wisely and you'll see your dreams become reality!

Step 8: Empowerment

A word that encompasses all of the reasons to activate your dreams and live a life of happiness. **The self-determination and power of choice is yours.** Take action steps that will give you options, increase your resources, and provide you a feeling of self-worth. You have permission to see your dreams come true and you deserve to experience the results of all your hard work. Empowerment is about all around wellness with a sense of peace that you did it your way. Congrats on activating your dreams!

Good Morning,

THE POWER OF TRUE LOVE is undeniable. There is no doubt, hesitation, or worry with True Love. There is absence of hate, selfishness, and ego when True Love is present. We long for the arrival and focus on sustaining that awesome feeling known as True Love. If we could give a little more and share a little more, we could heal the world with the only medicine needed...it's called True Love!

1. **What does True Love mean to you?**

2. **Think about someone who displayed True Love for you. How did impact you?**

Good Morning,

NEVER STOP DREAMING. OUR DREAMS **are the fuel to our life engine.** We must then put our physical vehicle on this road filled with ups and downs in order to reach our desired destinations. Some people will try to steal your dreams or make you believe that the journey is too difficult to navigate but it's your vision and your purpose to live. There is never failure in living your dreams, only lessons learned and success stories to share. Today's the day to let your dreams propel you. Enjoy your ride!

1. How is your engine running? Do you need a fill up?

2. What are 2 dreams you have for your life?

Good Morning,

IF WE MOVE WITH FEAR as our shadow, we live a life full of regret and disappointment. If we carry faith that's backed by focused action, we live a life full of purpose and satisfaction. Which will you choose?

1. **Don't let fear hold you back!**
2. **Live today with purpose and satisfaction.**

Good Morning,

IN A WORLD FILLED WITH noise, **learn how to quiet your mind.** Give yourself moments of escape throughout the day by focusing on peaceful, relaxing, and energizing thoughts. Don't let today's chaos steal your joy or run off with your peace of mind. We are currently in a state of busyness, which increases unhealthy stress and elevates anxiety responses to toxic levels. Seek calmness and clarity today. You will enjoy the feeling of mental freedom and the recharging of positive thoughts.

Practice mindfulness, which is the ability to be focused on the present with a peaceful and calming spirit.

Practice periods of escape with some peaceful imagery exercises. Think of a calming place or a peaceful sound.

Good Morning,

GROWTH DOES NOT TAKE PLACE **in a space of stagnation.** Change moves us to a place of discomfort in order for us to grow. In essence, the discomfort is the food that nourishes and prepares us for growth. It would seem that we should seek out opportunities to feel uncomfortable because that would communicate that we are stepping out of our comfort zones and stagnant mindsets that keep us from unlocking new doors of opportunity. Today is a day to chase discomfort. Move out of that comfort zone. Imagine how much you will grow because of it!

Name 3 areas that cause you some sort of discomfort. Why?

What are some ways you can grow and progress from these uncomfortable areas?

Good Morning,

TAKE TIME TO APPRECIATE THE wonderfulness of life. It's a beautiful journey we travel, with ups and downs that remind us to be humble. Let's appreciate every day, and do something that will positively impact the world. We can change the atmosphere with our positive energy. Give it a try.

Today I will appreciate my _____,
_____,and_____.

How can you positively impact the world today?

Good Morning,

You will have to inject a new action, a new mind-set, and a new focus into your daily journey. It's not enough to create a resolution that's designed with an old way of being. Goals do not get accomplished by simply stating a desire, only to use the same strategies that were unsuccessful in the past. It's time to decide to channel your energy with persistence. You must make daily steps toward achieving your goals and practice reflective evaluation. Make changes when needed, but keep moving forward. When you affirm that you will accomplish that goal, make sure you mean it with actions as well!

Keep your word, follow through with actions, and evaluate your progress.

Write down at least 2 actions steps for today.

Good Morning,

Go Crazy

Be fearless…Stand out…Walk away from the crowd…Let them talk about you…Be crazy…You're the weird one…Nobody believes you…That will never work…You can't do that…It will never work…Forget that idea. Take that negative energy and let it fuel you. People will call you crazy for chasing your dreams. Go crazy for your purpose. I'm not worried about the crazy dreamers. They'll always win!

Be bold when chasing your dreams. Be prepared for the ridicule but stand firm.

What does purpose mean to you? Describe your purpose in 3 words.

Good Morning,

The punches were positioned to knock you out, but only managed to knock you down. You were dazed and questioning whether you should even get up after that hit. It would have taken out the average or undetermined, but you reached. You reached so deep that you found something never discovered until now. A reach for resilience gave you a second wind. You got up and pushed through that obstacle, jumped that hurdle, and overcame that mountain. Your reach is more powerful than you know. Now you know how capable you and how strong you are. Reach for resilience when faced with a life battle…You're a fighter who has defeated bigger giants. Go win!

Think about a time in which you overcame a difficult challenge. How did it make you stronger?

The word resilience means a strong determination and fight to overcome a tough life obstacle.

Good Morning,

<u>Don't Fear the Jump!</u>

When you have taken that jump and fallen on your head several times, only to get back up even stronger… **you no longer have the same fear of the jump**, but you definitely have an intense anticipation for becoming stronger. Don't worry about the jump. Just be ready for the strength on the other side!

What is keeping you from taking that leap to reach your dreams?

Let your determination from past jumps be your assurance that you will be all right!

Good Morning,

Go places untraveled…Do what people say is impossible…Be more than extraordinary…Believe beyond the sun, moon, and stars…**Live a life that's full of happiness, compassion, and peace.**

Decide on a destination and make plans to travel there in the future.

What do happiness, compassion, and peace mean to you?

Good Morning,

It's just easier to look the other way and pretend everything is fine. You know that a change is needed but you have convinced yourself otherwise. The stress is screaming at you...The tough days just never seem to end. Listen to your feelings and face the signs. If you want better, you'll have to think better and do better. Sings are designed to be noticed! **If you notice something is off in your life, love yourself enough to make some changes to improve in those areas.** You deserve to be happy!

What signs are you ignoring in your life?

What changes do you need to make in your life to gain more happiness?

Good Morning,

Purpose, Position, Progress

There is a unique design for your life. A journey that is clearly created with your strengths, talents, and abilities in mind. Your **purpose** will continue to call you until you answer. **Position** yourself to follow your purpose. This requires a mindful eye and a determined spirit. Put yourself in the way of opportunities, but be prepared to create your own in order to move forward. Now it's time to understand **progress**, as you follow your purpose and position yourself for the win. Progress is movement along your journey. Failure is progress, ups are progress, and downs are also progress. See progress as a constant movement toward a goal, rather than some finite accomplishment or failure. **Follow your purpose, position yourself for the blessing, and progress along the way. It's a recipe for your success!**

Are you following the purpose for your life?

Are you putting yourself in position to receive the blessings and desires of your heart?

Just keep moving toward your goal, that's progress!

Good Morning,

You are worth the time, patience, understanding, and effort. You deserve the universe, so a promise of the stars is not enough. You can settle for mediocrity or demand the best. It's your choice, but knowing your worth will make it easy to decide. You can't talk down the price at a Rolls Royce Dealer. The value and quality are set. It's time to have the same attitude about your value. **Your worth is set. Never let someone devalue who you are.**

Write down 3 reasons why you are a valuable person.

Declare these values over your life every day and believe in yourself.

Good Morning,

BE READY FOR THE BLESSING!

True success does not happen by accident or some sort of crazy luck. Time, persistence, preparation, and energy are in the toolboxes of so many success builders. There is also another major component of success, which is the ability to be ready. Readiness encompasses a level of mindfulness, anticipation, and preparedness for the next door of opportunity. It also seems that a person who is ready is far from waiting. There is a "GO" mindset for success leaders, which is energetic and inspiring. **Be READY for your blessing. You never know when it may be your "GO" moment!**

What does true success mean to you?

Are you ready for your "GO" moment? What would that moment look like in your life?

Good Morning,

It may be scary to think about the greatness inside of you and the impact you can have on the world. Sometimes it's just easier to hide in a state of busyness. The cool thing about purpose is that it always finds you. Didn't you hate that as a kid? You played hide and go seek with friends, and everywhere you hid, it was always that one friend who found you. You kept saying, "Did you peek?" That's exactly what your purpose is doing. It's following you and you just can't hide. It keeps you awake, people ask about it, and you even dream about it. Stop hiding from your purpose. **The world needs to know who you are! You're someone with a purpose!**

Are you busy hiding or running away from your purpose? It's time to stop and face it!

Write down your purpose. Just start with some thoughts or statements. Now it's time to start your journey!

Final Thoughts

Now that you have completed your *Wake-Up Calls for Life* journey, it's time to rise and shine. You have learned so much about yourself along the way and are fully prepared to make some positive changes in your life. Some mornings may have revealed new insights into areas of strength, and some mornings may have shaken you a little in order to reveal areas that need improvement. The overall assessment is that you are growing as a person. You are utilizing the resiliency of previous battles and the appreciation from all of your triumphs.

This is just the beginning for you as you travel to new heights and new levels of fulfilling your purpose. Remember to show compassion to others and give whenever possible. This allows seeds of happiness to be planted and harvested by others along your purpose-driven path. I hope you are excited about the road ahead. I am definitely looking forward to connecting to the greatness you will bring to your families, friends, and communities. May God continue to grant you peace, health, and happiness along the way. May your Good Mornings continue, and may your Wake-Up Calls for Life be pleasant.

-Dr. Randolph D. Sconiers, DSW, LCSW

Written By: Dr. Randolph D. Sconiers, DSW, LCSW

Inspired by: Yinirda Martinez-Sconiers (my wife), Jazlyn, Destiny, Alina (my 3 beautiful daughters), Regina and Randolph Sconiers (my parents), and Adrienne Sconiers (my sister). Our bond is cemented and founded in relationships that only God could create. I love you guys! Thank you!

Thank you: To all my family and friends. Way too many to mention, but I truly appreciate all of your support and encouragement. My friends for life, Mars Stars, as our dreams have evolved from music, books, and film. We are talented and gifted in various ways. May we continue to shine!

57783946R10076

Made in the USA
Middletown, DE
03 August 2019